NOAH GETS NAKED

... and other fascinating Bible stories they don't teach you in Sunday School

GW00497023

by Xanna Eve Chown

For Lisa, always

Published by Doplin Books, Brighton, UK
www.doplinbooks.com

Text and illustrations copyright Xanna Eve Chown © 2018

With huge thanks to Paula, Sarah, Cara, Chrissie, Christine, Jo, and David. And especially to John.

CONTENTS

FURTHER READING

If you want to look up one of these stories,
a reference above each picture gives the name of
the Bible book it appears in, and a chapter number
to show you where to start reading.

PREFACE

The Christian Bible has two sections: the Old Testament and the New Testament. The Old Testament is like a library, containing over thirty books of law, history, poetry, prophecy, and wisdom, written between 1200 and 100 BC. It corresponds to the Tanakh, a collection of Jewish sacred scriptures.

Many Old Testament stories are well-known, but you won't find any of *them* in this book, because **Noah Gets Naked** aims to give you a glimpse of the world beyond the Ark. Did you know, for example...

... that God gave a donkey the gift of speech?
... that Moses was allowed to see God's bottom?
... or that Samson's fiancée married his Best Man?

Well, you do now! Read on to find out more fascinating stories from the world's most famous book — from the quirky and confusing to the bloodthirsty and downright bizarre.

The Old Testament Story
(abridged)

1) God Creates The World

God created the first people: Adam and Eve. Some time later, he sent a flood to kill everyone on Earth except their great-great-great-great-great-great-great grandson Noah.

Noah Gets Naked – page 8

2) The First Israelites

Noah's great-great-great-great-great-great-great-great grandson Abraham was the first prophet. His grandson Israel (AKA Jacob) was the ancestor of the Israelites, God's favourite people. Jacob and his family moved to Egypt when his son Joseph (of technicolour dreamcoat fame) got a job working for the Pharoah.

The Salty Wife – page 10

3) Escape From Egypt

The Israelites were slaves in Egypt for a long time, then God helped the prophet Moses set them free. Moses led the Israelites to the Promised Land of Canaan. Unfortunately, he died before they got there, because the journey took forty years.

God's Bottom – page 12
Drowning In Quail – page 14

4) The Promised Land

The problem with the Israelites settling in Canaan was that people already lived there. These people worshipped false gods such as Baal and Dagon, so God helped the Israelites to defeat them.

The Talking Donkey – page 16

5) The Era Of Judges

The Israelites were constantly being oppressed by other nations, including the Moabites, Philistines, Canaanites, and Ammonites. When the going got tough, they were led by Judges, such as Ehud, Jephthah, Deborah and Samson.

6) The Rule Of Kings

The Israelites became jealous of the other nations' kings, so God gave them King Saul, King David and King Solomon. After Solomon died, there was a civil war.

7) The Kingdom Divided

The kingdom split in two: Israel and Judah. Each had their own king.

8) Judah And Israel Fall

First Israel fell to the Assyrians, then Judah to the Babylonians. The Israelites were captured and many taken into slavery.

9) The Israelites Return

The people taken by the Assyrians were lost, but the ones taken by the Babylonians were allowed home after the Persians conquered Babylon.

GENESIS 9

NOAH GETS NAKED

Adam and Eve were the first people to live on Earth, but it was a time of angels, giants and heroes, and before long there were people everywhere, behaving very badly.

God decided to start again. He sent a flood to kill everyone except Adam's great-great-great-great-great-great-great grandson Noah, and his family.

Although Noah is most famous as an animal conservationist, he was a farmer, and when the floodwater had finally gone down, he planted a vineyard and made some wine. The wine was very tasty, and Noah did not share it. Feeling rather tipsy, he went into his tent, took off all his clothes, and fell asleep.

Noah's son, Ham, peeped into the tent, then sped off to tell his brothers, Shem and Japheth, what he had seen. They were not so easily amused. They found a cloak to cover their father, and walked backwards as they carried it, to make sure that they didn't see anything they shouldn't.

Noah woke up with a headache and a prophetic vision.

He blessed Shem and Japheth for what they had done, but can you guess who he cursed? Surprise! It was Ham's son, Canaan. And his descendants, the Canaanites too, for good measure.

GENESIS 19

THE SALTY WIFE

The city of Sodom was so sinful that God decided to destroy it. But first, he sent two angels to see if they could find any good men living there at all. The angels found Lot, who was Noah's great-great-great-great-great-great-great-great grandson, and good-ish.

Word spread through Sodom that two beautiful strangers were having dinner at Lot's house, and it wasn't long before every man in the city was banging on the door, demanding to see them. Lot knew that they planned to do more than just look at his guests, so he offered to send out his two daughters instead.

Sadly for him, the men of Sodom were not interested in girls. 'We'll break down the door!' they shouted.

'You have to find it first,' replied the angels, and blinded the men. The angels told Lot's family to flee the city and not look back.

Lot's wife could be forgiven for thinking this was a figure of speech. But it wasn't. As fire rained down on Sodom, she stopped to look and was instantly turned into a pillar of salt.

Lot took his daughters, and a large quantity of wine, and went to live in a cave. This is how, nine months later, he became both father and grandfather to two boys – the ancestors of the Israelites' enemies, the Moabites and Ammonites.

EXODUS 33

GOD'S BOTTOM

The Israelites were slaves in Egypt for a long time, and it wasn't much fun. Luckily, they were God's favourite people, and he eventually sent the prophet Moses to set them free.

Moses had a great relationship with God, and everyone knew it. When God talked to Moses, a tall pillar of cloud hovered at the entrance of the meeting tent that was always put aside for their chats.

So, God was probably a little surprised when, one day, Moses asked him if their relationship really was special.

'Of course it is,' said God.

'But you always talk to me from the cloud,' grumbled Moses. 'And *everyone* can see the cloud. I want to see what you *really* look like.'

'Oh dear,' said God. 'I'd like to show you, but I'm afraid that no one can see my face and live.' Then he had an idea. 'Stand on this rock,' he said. 'I will put you in a crack and cover you with my hand while I pass by in all my glory. Then I'll take my hand away and you can see me – from the back.'

So that's what they did.

And that is how Moses became the only man on record to be allowed to catch a glimpse of God's bottom.

NUMBERS 11

DROWNING IN QUAIL

The Israelites wandered in the wilderness for forty years after escaping from Egypt. But they never went hungry because God sent magical flakes that fell from the sky and tasted like coriander. The Israelites called it 'manna', which means 'what is it?'

Sadly, even magical food gets boring after a while.

'We used to eat *fish* when we lived in Egypt,' moaned the Israelites. 'And cucumbers. And melons. And leeks and onions and garlic. Now all we see is *manna*. We want meat!'

'I'll give you meat till it comes out of your nostrils,' God said angrily. What could he mean?

Suddenly, a wind blew in from the sea. The sky darkened and millions of tiny birds began raining down on the Israelites. *Plop! Plop! Plop!* They fell until the camp was covered in a blanket of quail, about a metre deep.

The Israelites waded through the birds all day and night, gathering up more than they could possibly eat. But as they stuffed themselves with meat, a wave of food poisoning swept through the camp. The Israelites were sick until the quail they'd eaten spurted out of their noses, and many died.

Nobody likes a whiner, and God is no exception.

NUMBERS 22

THE TALKING DONKEY

The King of the Moabites was afraid of the Israelites. He sent messengers to the prophet Balaam, asking him to curse them.

Being a sensible chap, Balaam replied that he would have to check with God first.

God said no.

The messengers didn't want any trouble, so they asked Balaam to come to the palace and tell the King his answer in person.

Balaam agreed, but when they set off, God sent an angel with a sharp sword to block their path.

Hee-haw! Balaam's donkey veered off the road and into a field. But Balaam couldn't see the angel, so he hit the donkey and forced her back onto the road. This happened again and again until, finally, the donkey lay down and refused to move.

Then, God gave the donkey the gift of speech.

'Why do you keep *hitting* me?' she brayed.

'She saved your life,' said the angel.

At last, Balaam could see the angel. He fell to his knees, praising God – and when the angel told him to go to Moab and bless the Israelites, he agreed at once. He knew he'd had a lucky escape and felt grateful. What the donkey felt has not been recorded.

JUDGES 3

THE VERY FAT KING

King Eglon the Corpulent was not very nice to the Israelites, and after eighteen years, they'd had enough. A brave, left-handed man called Ehud hid a small sword under his clothes and went to the King's roof chamber.

'I have a secret message for you,' said Ehud. 'It's from God.'

When the King heard this, he sent his servants out of the room so he could listen to the message in private.

Big mistake. Huge. A bit like King Eglon.

Ehud plunged his sharp sword into the King's wobbly belly. The handle sank in after the blade, the fat closed over the top and Eglon began to poop. Then, Ehud hurried away to tell the Israelites what had happened, locking the doors behind him.

After he had gone, the servants discovered that the doors were locked. 'The King must be using the royal toilet,' they said.

They waited for a long time, until they felt very embarrassed. At last someone fetched a key to unlock the doors, and there was the King, dead on the floor.

To add insult to injury, while the servants cleaned up what must have been a pretty nasty mess, the Israelite army captured Eglon's kingdom, killing ten thousand men.

JUDGES 4

TENT PEG IN THE HEAD

Sisera was a Canaanite general. He had nine hundred iron chariots and he used them all to oppress the Israelites. After twenty years, God decided to help. He sent the prophet Deborah with a message for Barak, the leader of the Israelite army.

'Go to Mount Tabor,' she said. 'God will help you defeat Sisera.'

Barak looked nervous. 'I'll go if you come with me,' he said.

Deborah agreed to go, but with a chilling prophecy. 'God will give the glory of Sisera's death to a *woman* instead of you.'

The Israelites marched to Mount Tabor and everything went according to plan. God flooded a river, and all Sisera's chariots were swept away. Sisera fled to the tent of a woman called Jael, whose husband was a friend of the Canaanites.

'Come in, my lord,' said Jael, sweetly. She gave Sisera a blanket and a cup of milk and promised to keep watch over him. But as soon as he was asleep, she picked up a mallet and drove a tent peg through his head and into the ground.

When Deborah heard the news, she was so pleased that she started to sing. 'She struck Sisera, she crushed his head, she shattered and pierced his temple,' she warbled happily. 'Most blessed of women be Jael!' Her prophecy had come true.

JUDGES 11

DADDY'S GIRL

Jephthah was an Israelite soldier who made a rather rash promise to God. 'Please help me defeat the Ammonite army,' he prayed. 'If you do, I'll give you the first thing that comes out of my house when I get home – as a burnt offering.'

It probably seemed like a good idea at the time.

Jephthah went to the land of the Ammonites and God helped him defeat them. Then he returned home.

As he approached his house, his only daughter came dancing out to congratulate him on his victory, playing her tambourine.

'Oh no!' Jephthah cried. He loved his daughter very much. 'I made a promise to God and I can't change it.'

'If you make a promise to God, you must keep it,' said his daughter, piously. 'What did you promise?'

Jephthah told her everything.

'Ah,' said his daughter. 'Well, in that case, I would like to go to the mountains for two months with my friends, to mourn the future I have lost.'

Jephthah let her go. He tore his clothes and wept to show how sad he was, but of course, when his daughter came home, he kept his promise, and burned her to death.

JUDGES 14

THREE HUNDRED FLAMING FOXES

Samson was the strongest of all the Israelites. One day, he found bees making honey in the body of a lion he'd killed, and it inspired him to write a riddle: *Out of the eater came something to eat. Out of the strong came something sweet.*

Samson was in love with a Philistine girl. On his wedding day, he told the riddle to his Philistine guests and offered thirty sets of clothes to anyone who guessed it correctly.

The guests paid a visit to Samson's bride. 'Tell us the answer or we'll burn down your house,' they said. She told them the answer.

Samson was furious. He stormed off and killed thirty random Philistines, taking their bloody clothes to the guests to pay his debt. Then he went back home to live with his parents.

Time passed, and Samson decided to visit his bride's village. But when he got there, she had married his Best Man.

'Sorry,' her father said. 'We thought you hated her now. Why don't you marry her sister instead? She's prettier.'

But Samson didn't want marriage; he wanted revenge. So, he caught three hundred foxes, tied their tails together with burning torches, and threw them into the Philistines' cornfields. I'm sure you'd have done exactly the same if you were in his situation.

I SAMUEL 5

FIVE GOLDEN HAEMORRHOIDS

The Israelites had a holy box called the Ark of the Covenant. One day, the Philistines stole it, and put it in the temple of a fish-god called Dagon. God was not at all pleased. He gave the Philistines haemorrhoids which made their bottoms itchy, and sent a plague of mice too for good measure.

'The Ark must go!' cried the Philistines.

'Yes,' said their priests, who were suffering too. 'Let's send it back to the Israelites with an offering for their God.'

The Philistines made five haemorrhoids and five mice out of gold and loaded them onto a cart with the Ark.

'Fetch two cows that have just given birth,' said the priests. 'If they pull the cart back to their calves, we'll know that all these problems were caused by bad luck, not God.' But the cows pulled the cart to the Israelites, mooing all the way, so that was settled.

The Israelites were so happy that they began to celebrate, singing and dancing and making sacrifices. Then, some of them decided to look inside the Ark – even though it was forbidden and they really should have known better.

God didn't waste time punishing them with haemorrhoids or mice, though. He killed all the peeping Israelites on the spot.

I SAMUEL 28

THE WITCH OF ENDOR

The Israelites were about to fight the Philistines and their leader, King Saul, was afraid. God used to help him win battles – but God wasn't talking to him any more.

'If only the prophet Samuel hadn't died,' muttered King Saul. 'He'd be able to tell me what was going on.' Then he had a marvellous idea. He could make a witch conjure up Samuel's ghost for him.

It took the King a while to find a witch, as he had recently banned them all from the land. But at last, he heard of one living in Endor and visited her in disguise.

The witch saw the ghost of an old man in a robe rising up from the ground, and King Saul knew it was Samuel.

'Why are you bothering me?' asked the ghost, peevishly.

'I think God has left me,' said the King.

'Of *course* he's left you,' snapped the ghost. 'You stopped obeying him. You'll lose tomorrow's battle *and* you will die.'

King Saul fainted, and the witch had to cook him a meal of bread and beef to revive him. He didn't want to leave her house, and who can blame him? He died the next day in battle, just like the grumpy spirit had predicted.

2 SAMUEL 14

HANGING BY HIS HAIR

King David had a handsome son called Absalom, who was very proud of his long hair. He had it cut once a year, and it weighed two hundred shekels. That's about the same as a chihuahua in modern terms.

Absalom hatched a plot to overthrow his father and gathered an army to help him. King David was taken by surprise and fled the city, leaving ten of his wives behind to take care of the palace. Absalom claimed the palace, the crown and all ten wives for himself, while his father camped outside the city and prepared for war.

The rebellion ended when the two armies met in Ephraim Forest. Absalom was riding under a large oak tree when his long, luxurious hair got caught in the branches. His horse bolted, and he was left hanging in mid-air. No matter how hard he tried, he couldn't get free.

Before long, King David's soldiers found him, and stuck three spears into his heart. They threw his body into a hole in the ground and covered it with stones. If only Absalom had managed to have one of his famous haircuts before the battle, things might have turned out very differently.

I KINGS 18

BAAL IN THE BATHROOM

One day, the prophet Elijah challenged four hundred and fifty priests of Baal to a contest at the top of Mount Carmel. He told them to sacrifice a bull and place it on an altar.

'Now ask Baal to light the fire under it,' he said.

So, the priests yelled Baal's name for hours, dancing wildly around the altar, but nothing happened.

'I don't think Baal can hear you,' said Elijah, clearly enjoying himself. 'Perhaps he's busy? Or taking a nap? Wait, do you think he had to go to the *toilet*?'

The priests shouted louder and slashed their bodies with spears and swords until blood flowed, but it was no use.

Then it was Elijah's turn. He was so confident that God would answer him, he even splashed his firewood with water before he started praying.

God's flames fell from heaven as soon as he spoke.

'Praise God!' cried the watching Israelites, who knew a sign when they saw it.

Before the priests had a chance to say, 'Best of three?' Elijah commanded the Israelites to take the priests of Baal down to the valley and kill them all. (And they did.)

EATEN BY DOGS

Queen Jezebel was beautiful but cruel. For example, she once had a man killed because he wouldn't sell her his vegetable garden.

Her husband, King Ahab of Israel, worshipped God, but she encouraged him to worship nature gods too, such as Baal and Asherah. God did not approve of this kind of behaviour, and sent a host of disasters to destroy the royal family.

King Ahab died in battle and his son, Ahaziah, took the throne. Ahaziah had a nasty fall from a latticed window and was replaced by his brother, who was killed in a coup by his general, Jehu.

When Queen Jezebel heard that Jehu was on his way to the palace, she knew he planned to kill her, too. But she didn't run away. She put on make-up, fixed her hair and greeted him calmly from one of the palace windows.

Jehu ordered her servants to throw her down to him.

The Queen fell to her death, blood spattering the wall and the horses below. Jehu drove his chariot over her body, then went into the palace to eat.

By the time he had finished his meal, there was nothing left of the Queen but her skull, her feet and the palms of her hands.

The rest had been licked up by stray dogs.

2 KINGS 2

BALDY AND THE BEARS

God loved the prophet Elijah, and when the time came for him to die, God sent a chariot of fire and a whirlwind to take him up to Heaven. His disciple, the prophet Elisha, saw it all, and went to the city of Jericho to tell the other prophets what had happened.

'What if God dropped him on top of a mountain?' they exclaimed, and suggested sending out a search party.

Elisha told them not to, but they went on and on about it until he couldn't take any more, and let them send fifty men.

The men searched for three days and came back empty handed.

'I told you not to go,' said Elisha, testily.

Elisha travelled to the city of Bethel. As he was walking up the hill, a gang of boys came out and began to laugh and jeer at him. 'Go away, Baldy! Go away, Baldy!' they chanted rudely.

Elisha turned and gave them a hard stare, then cursed them in the name of God. At once, two female bears came out of the woods and they tore forty-two of the boys to bits.

The lesson here, of course, is that you should never tease a prophet. But perhaps it's a good idea to be nice to bald people too, just to be on the safe side.

2 CHRONICLES 22

THE MURDEROUS GRANNY

A death in the family can affect people in different ways. For example, when King Ahaziah of Judah died, his mother Athaliah sent her guards to kill all his children.

With the heirs to the throne out of the way, Athaliah became Queen. She had no idea that one grandchild had survived.

Baby Joash was smuggled out of the palace by the King's sister during all the commotion. He was taken to the temple and lived there for six years with the priest, Jehoiada.

When Joash was seven years old, the priest decided that the time was right for a rebellion. He sent for the palace guards and introduced them to their rightful ruler.

'Long live the King!' shouted the guards, who were fed up with Queen Athaliah. The people who heard them started to celebrate, blowing trumpets and singing.

The Queen heard the noise and rushed to the Temple. To her amazement, she saw a coronation taking place.

'This is treason!' she screamed, as her guards turned on her.

Jehoiada told the guards not to kill the Queen in the Temple, because it was a holy place. So they took her to a palace gate called the 'Horse Gate' and killed her there instead.

ESTHER I

QUEEN VASHTI SAYS NO

King Ahasuerus of Persia was rich and powerful, and he wanted everyone to know it. He threw a party at his palace which lasted for one hundred and eighty days and, when it was over, invited all the men to stay for a banquet.

'Look at my beautiful things,' the King ordered.

So the guests wondered at his mosaic pavements (made of marble and mother-of-pearl), marvelled at his couches (made of gold and silver), and drank wine from his patterned cups. But the banquet lasted for a week and the King ran out of things for his guests to admire. That was when he remembered his wife.

'Bring the Queen to me,' he told his servants. 'Wearing her royal crown,' he added with a wink.

But Queen Vashti refused to go.

'If other women hear about this, they will *all* stop obeying their husbands!' gasped the palace officials.

Everyone agreed this would be a very bad thing, so the King issued a royal decree, banning Queen Vashti from seeing him again – and I'm sure you know what that meant.

That's right! Poor Ahasuerus had to go to all the bother of finding himself another wife.

EZEKIEL 3

A FIRE OF HUMAN POOP

One time, when the Israelites were being particularly sinful, God decided to destroy the city of Jerusalem. He chose the prophet Ezekiel to tell the Israelites in Babylon about his plans, through the somewhat unlikely medium of performance art.

First, God gave Ezekiel a scroll covered in sad words, and told him to swallow it. Luckily, it tasted like honey.

Then, he told Ezekiel to scratch a picture of Jerusalem on a brick and build a dirt wall around it and a dirt road leading up to it. 'Pretend you are an army surrounding the city,' God said. 'Take an iron pan and put it between you and the brick. Roll up your sleeve and raise your arm over it.'

Next, he commanded Ezekiel to lie on his left side for three hundred and ninety days, and his right side for forty days. 'I'll tie you down so you can't roll over,' he added helpfully. All this time, Ezekiel could only eat bread made from wheat, barley, beans, lentils and millet, baked on a fire made from human poop.

Even Ezekiel thought this was a step too far. 'Please don't make me do that,' he said.

'Very well,' said God, kindly. 'You can make the fire with cow dung instead.'

DANIEL 4

THE KING WHO ATE GRASS

King Nebuchadnezzar of Babylon had a strange dream. He sent for the prophet Daniel to ask him what it meant.

'I saw a tree that was tall and strong,' the King said. 'But an angel told me to cut it down, leaving the roots and stump behind.'

'That dream is a message from God,' Daniel said. 'He thinks you're too proud. He plans to make you live like an animal until you realise that *he* is the one in charge.'

Daniel begged the King to change his ways, but it was no use, and just one year later, the prophecy came true.

Nebuchadnezzar was walking on the flat roof of his palace, looking proudly down at the city below. 'I built this,' he said. 'My, oh my, what a powerful ruler I am!'

Suddenly, the King's hair started to grow until it was as long as an eagle's feathers, and his nails became as long as an bird's claws. He fell to his knees and chomped at the grass like a cow, until his servants drove him away to live with the animals in the fields.

It was seven years before God restored the King's mind and Nebuchanezzar could go back to ruling Babylon as he had before. But this time, the King spent a *lot* more time praising God – and who can blame him?

DANIEL 5

GOD'S GRAFFITI

King Belshazzar of Babylon invited one thousand lords to his palace for a party. The tables were laid with the cups that his father, Nebuchadnezzar, had stolen from the Israelites. As the guests ate and drank, they praised statues made of gold, silver, bronze, iron, wood and stone. What a great party! No one could have guessed what was about to happen.

Suddenly, a human hand appeared in the air and started to scratch four mysterious words into the plaster wall, near the lampstand: *Mene, Mene, Tekel, Upharsin.*

The King was so scared that he turned white and his knees began to knock. He promised to reward anyone who could explain what these strange words meant.

The Queen sent for the prophet Daniel.

'I'm so sorry,' Daniel said politely. 'You're doomed. God isn't pleased with you at all, and he plans to give your kingdom to the Persians.'

The King was killed that night, and his kingdom was taken by the Persians. He had heaped rewards and honours on Daniel, but there was nothing anyone could do to change his fate.

If it's not clear by now: God always has the last word.

COMING SOON:

JESUS AND THE DEMON PIGS

Bible Stories They Didn't Teach In Sunday School
- Part 2: The New Testament -

ADAM AND EVE (AND LILITH)

The Stories That *Almost* Made It Into The Bible
- Tales From The Apocrypha -

BABY JESUS HEALS A DEAD FISH

Strange Stories From Jesus's Childhood
- From The Infancy Gospel Of Thomas -

Printed in Great Britain
by Amazon